COUNTRIES IN OUR WORLD

ISRAEL

Andrew Langley

FRANKLIN WATTS
LONDON • SYDNEY

First published in 2010 by
Franklin Watts
338 Euston Road
London NW1 3BH

Franklin Watts Australia
Level 17/207 Kent Street
Sydney NSW 2000

Produced for Franklin Watts by
White-Thomson Publishing Ltd
+44 (0) 843 208 7460
www.wtpub.co.uk

Series consultant: Rob Bowden
Editor: Sonya Newland
Designer: Clare Nicholas
Picture researcher: Amy Sparks

A CIP catalogue record for this book is available
from the British Library.

Dewey Classification: 956.9'4054

ISBN 978 0 7496 9201 8

Printed in Malaysia

Franklin Watts is a division of Hachette Children's
Books, an Hachette UK company

www.hachette.co.uk

Picture Credits
Corbis: 7 (Bettmann), 9 (Jon Arnold/JAI), 13 (Gil
Cohen Magen), 15 (Serge Attal/Sygma), 17 (Vicky
Alhadeff/Lebrecht Music & Arts), 18 (Antoine
Gyori/Sygma), 20 (Eldad Rafaeli), 23 (Reuters),
24 (Yossi Zamir/epa), 25 (Nati Shohat/Flash90/
Reuters), 26 (Ibraheem Abu Mustafa/Reuters),
27 (Abed al Hashlamoun/epa), 28 (Jose Manual
Vidal/epa); **Dreamstime:** 22 (Arkadiy Yarmalenko);
Photolibrary: 5 (Fabian von Poser), 10 (Jon Arnold);
Shutterstock: Cover (Dejan Gileski), 1 (Shootov Igor),
6 (Yuri Gershberg), 8 (Shootov Igor), 11 (Ivan
Roslyakov), 12 (Ryan Rodrick Beiler), 14 (Rudolf),
16 (Mikhail Levit), 19 (Nir Keidar), 21 (Liu Jixing),
29 (Nir Levy).

Contents

▷ Introducing Israel 4

► Landscapes and environment 8

▷ Population and migration 12

► Culture and lifestyles 16

▷ Economy and trade 20

► Government and politics 24

▷ Israel in 2020 28

► Glossary 30

▷ Further information 31

► Index 32

Israel is a small country in south-west Asia, on the eastern shore of the Mediterranean Sea. It has a wide variety of landscapes, including mountains, deserts, fertile valleys and coastline.

Arab neighbours

Israel has borders with four countries – Lebanon to the north, Syria and Jordan to the east, and Egypt to the south-west. All of them are Arab states, whose people are mostly followers of the Islamic faith. But some parts of Israel's borders are not easy to define. In wars since 1948, Israel has seized large areas of territory from its neighbours. Among them are the West Bank of the River Jordan and the Gaza Strip, home to Palestinian Arabs. Despite many years of talks and protests, no decision has been made about the future of these areas, which are known as the Palestinian Territories.

▶ *Israel borders the Mediterranean Sea in the west. It also has short stretches of coastline along the landlocked Dead Sea in the east and the Red Sea in the south.*

LEBANON

SYRIA

Sea of Galilee

Haifa ○

Mediterranean Sea

Tel Aviv ○

WEST BANK

River Jordan

Jerusalem ■

GAZA STRIP

○ Sderot

Dead Sea

Masada ○

I S R A E L

JORDAN

N E G E V

D E S E R T

EGYPT

Key
■ Capital city
○ Other cities

Eilat ○

```
0          miles          50
0        kilometres      50
```

Red Sea

SAUDI ARABIA

The birth of Israel

Modern Israel covers much the same area as the ancient Kingdom of Israel described in the Bible. This was where the faith called Judaism began nearly 4,000 years ago. When the Romans conquered the region in CE 63 they called it Palestine. Over the centuries, the Jews were driven out and scattered across the world. It was not until 1948 that Israel was created as a national Jewish home. Palestine was divided into two states – one for Jews and one for Palestinian Arabs.

IT'S A FACT!

Israel is the only Jewish state in the world. It was founded in 1948 as a homeland for the Jewish people. Today, about three out of every four Israelis are Jews. The rest of the population are mainly Arabs and Muslim.

▼ *The ruins of the 2,000-year-old fortress at Masada overlook the desert and the Dead Sea.*

A violent history

The division of Palestine made many Arab
governments angry. They believed the
Palestinian Arabs had been robbed of their
homeland. Armies from five Arab countries
launched an invasion in 1948, aimed at
destroying the new state of Israel. There have
been several wars between the two sides since
then. Israel, heavily supported by the USA,
has usually been the winner, but the violence
goes on. In 2000, the Palestinians began a fresh
uprising against Israel. This led to an Israeli invasion
of Gaza in 2009. At least 6,000 people on both sides
were killed in this latest conflict.

BASIC DATA

Official name: **State of Israel**

Capital: **Jerusalem**

Size: **20,770 sq km (7,849 sq miles)**

Population: **7,233,701**

Currency: **Israeli new shekel**

▼ *Israeli soldiers in Sderot, a city
close to the Gaza Strip. The Israeli
army invaded the region in 2009.*

▲ *Jewish immigrants arriving in Israel in 1948, the first of a million settlers that would arrive there in the next 10 years.*

IT STARTED HERE

Judaism

The Jewish religion is one of the oldest in the world. It was founded nearly 4,000 years ago by the Hebrew leader Abraham in the land that is now Israel. Jews believe that there is one God, and that a person should study the scriptures and practise what they teach. Judaism has spread to many parts of the world, and now has about 13 million followers.

A flood of immigrants

Many Jews came to Palestine from Europe and the USSR in the 1930s to escape persecution, but after the foundation of the new state, immigrants arrived in even greater numbers. Over one million Jews settled in Israel between 1948 and 1958. They have since been followed by nearly two million more. Because these immigrants have come from many countries, they share a religion but have their own traditions and language.

Israel has four main land areas. The largest is the Negev Desert in the south. East of this is the narrow and steep-sided Rift Valley, and to the north are the highlands, including the mountains of Galilee. The Coastal Plain is a thin strip of land next to the Mediterranean.

Beside the sea

For a small state, Israel has a long coastline. The Coastal Plain is the most fertile farmland in the country. Most farming and industry is located here, and so are many of Israel's biggest towns. Haifa, in the north, is the country's major port and a vital trading link with Mediterranean cargo routes. Israel also has a small stretch of Red Sea coastline in the far south, which gives it an important outlet into the Indian Ocean.

▲ *Situated on the Mediterranean coast, the port of Haifa is a vital link for trade with other countries.*

Israel's climate

Israel generally has cool winters and hot, dry summers. The coldest areas are in the highlands, where the highest mountain tops are often covered in snow for most of the year. The hottest places are the lowland desert areas around the Dead Sea and in the Negev Desert. Temperatures here can reach 49°C (120°F). The Sun shines almost continuously across Israel between May and mid-October. Almost all the rain falls between November and March, though the driest parts of the Negev Desert receive an average of only 5 cm (2 in) of rain a year.

IT'S A FACT!

Spring often sees a very hot dry wind blowing through Israel from the east. This is called *khamsin*. It brings huge amounts of sand and dust from the deserts, and can travel at more than 140 km/h (87 mph).

▶ *In the dry Negev Desert, the wind has worn the stone into strange shapes like this 'mushroom' in the Timna National Park area of the desert.*

Fresh water

The Jordan is the longest river in Israel, and is an important source of fresh water. It runs from the northern borders for 360 km (223 miles). On the way, it flows through a large lake called the Sea of Galilee. Water is pumped from here to help grow crops on farmland in the dry area to the west. The Jordan runs on southwards and empties into the Dead Sea.

▼ *The Jordan – Israel's longest river – flows through the Sea of Galilee in the north-east.*

PLACE IN THE WORLD

Total area: **20,770 sq km (7,849 sq miles)**

Percentage of world land area: **0.013%**

World ranking: **152nd**

Environmental issues

Israel is a small country with limited supplies of fresh water, but it is also growing fast, with expanding towns, industry and agriculture. This creates big environmental problems. As more water is taken from rivers to irrigate crops, the rivers themselves shrink. The Dead Sea has shrunk by 33 per cent in the last 50 years. At the same time, the air is polluted by fumes from factories and vehicles, and water sources are polluted by factory waste and chemical fertilizers used on farmland.

IT'S A FACT!

The Dead Sea is the lowest point on the face of the Earth. Its surface is 422 m (1,385 ft) below sea level. It is also one of the saltiest lakes in the world – its water contains about 33 per cent salt.

▼ *As Israel's towns and cities grow, factories and power plants pump more and more pollution into the air and nearby water sources.*

Population and migration

The population of Israel has grown very quickly. In 1948, the region had about 0.8 million inhabitants. Since then, the total has shot up to over 7.2 million. The vast majority of these people live in the towns and cities, especially on the Coastal Plain. The least densely populated area is the Negev Desert.

The people of Israel

There are two major ethnic groups in Israel – Jews and Arabs. The largest of these is the Jews, who make up more than 75 per cent of the population. Most of them are the families of immigrants who have arrived since 1948 from all over the world. The rest of the population are mostly Arabs, descendants of the Palestinians who lived in the area before Israel became an independent state. Over three million Arabs also live in the Palestinian Territories of Gaza and the West Bank. The Israeli army controls these areas, but they are not officially part of Israel.

IT'S A FACT!

The Palestinian Territories (Gaza and the West Bank) are more than twice as crowded as Israel. In Israel, the population density is 302 people per sq km (780 per sq mile). In the Palestinian Territories there are 667 people per sq km (1,780 per sq mile).

◀ *Israeli soldiers pass an Arab woman on the streets of Jerusalem. The Israeli army has a presence in the big cities as well as the Palestinian Territories.*

Major cities

Jerusalem is Israel's capital and its largest city, with a population of over 747,000. It is divided into two parts. West Jerusalem is the Jewish area, while East Jerusalem is inhabited mainly by Arabs. Israelis captured East Jerusalem during a war in 1967, and now claim the whole city as their capital. International bodies such as the United Nations (UN) do not agree with this claim. Israel's other large cities are Tel Aviv, which is the main industrial centre, and Haifa, the country's biggest port.

▲ *People pass the time on the streets of Tel Aviv, the second-largest city in Israel, with a population of nearly 400,000.*

PLACE IN THE WORLD

Population: **7,233,701**

Percentage of world total: **0.10%**

World ranking: **98th**

Zionism

For centuries, Jews all over the world dreamed of returning to their ancient homeland, which they called Zion. In the 1880s, a Zionist movement began in Europe, encouraging Jews to emigrate to Palestine. Over the next 50 years, waves of Jewish immigrants arrived there. Many were escaping persecution, especially in Russia, Germany and Eastern Europe. After 1948, the number of immigrants grew rapidly. Over one million Jews came from Europe after the collapse of the Soviet Union in the early 1990s. In recent times, large numbers have migrated from countries as far apart as Ethiopia, China, Romania and the USA.

GOING GLOBAL

Where have Jewish immigrants come from since 1948?

Asia	0.4 million
Africa	0.5 million
Europe	1.7 million
America/Oceania	0.2 million
World total	2.8 million

▼ *The Western Wall in Jerusalem is an ancient place of worship for Jews. Close by is the golden Dome of the Rock, one of the most important places of Muslim worship.*

The effects of immigration

The arrival of so many Jewish settlers in such a short time has brought huge change to Israel. The immigrants needed houses and jobs, as well as food, healthcare and education. Israel has had to develop very quickly to cope with the demand. But this rapid change has created problems for some Israelis, especially the Arab population. Thanks to the flood of immigrants, Arabs now make up less than a quarter of the population. They have lost large areas of land as well as political power, and many feel angry and bitter.

▲ *There are more than five million Jews in the USA, the largest population of Jews outside Israel.*

Jews abroad

There are still large Jewish communities in countries outside Israel. The biggest, numbering over five million, is in the USA, many of them in New York. Many Jews have also settled in Canada, Argentina and Brazil. In Europe, the biggest communities can be found in France, Germany and the UK. Up to one million Jews live in the countries of the former Soviet Union, which include Russia.

Israeli society contains a huge variety of people. The immigrants who make up a large part of the population come from many different parts of the world. They have different customs and languages, and even different ways of practising their Jewish faith. The Arabs, who are mainly Muslims, also live in a very different way from Jewish Israelis.

THE HOME OF...

The kibbutz

About half of people in rural Israel live on a kibbutz. This is a farming community where members share the work and the property. In exchange for their labour on the land, they get food, housing, education and medical care. The idea of the kibbutz was pioneered in Palestine 100 years ago.

Religion

For centuries, the area covered by modern Israel has been a holy place for three major religions. Jews, Christians and Muslims all believe that certain places there are sacred. Because the majority of Israelis are Jews, Israel is not just a homeland for Jews but is also the most important centre for Judaism in the world. Most Israeli Arabs (about 16 per cent of the population) are Muslims, although some belong to a separate Islamic sect called the Druze. There is also a small number of Christians (about two per cent).

◀ *These Christians are celebrating the annual Miracle of Holy Fire in the Church of the Holy Sepulchre in Jerusalem.*

FAMOUS ISRAELI

Daniel Barenboim (b. 1942)

Barenboim is one of the world's great classical pianists. He gave his first public concert when he was only seven and his family moved to Israel in 1952. He went on to become a famous musician and conductor in Europe and the USA. He has worked hard to build better relations between Israelis and Palestinians, and has set up an Arab-Israeli orchestra (see page 28).

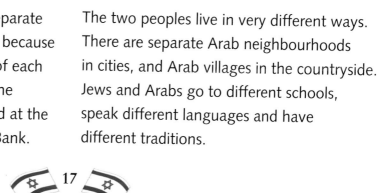

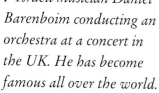

▶ *Israeli musician Daniel Barenboim conducting an orchestra at a concert in the UK. He has become famous all over the world.*

Separate lives

Most Jews and Arabs in Israel lead separate lives, with little contact. This is partly because the two communities are suspicious of each other. Many Arabs are still angry at the establishment of the Jewish state, and at the Israeli actions in Gaza and the West Bank.

The two peoples live in very different ways. There are separate Arab neighbourhoods in cities, and Arab villages in the countryside. Jews and Arabs go to different schools, speak different languages and have different traditions.

▲ *These young boys are studying Hebrew at school, the ancient language of the Jews.*

FAMOUS ISRAELI

Natalie Portman (b. 1981)

The actress Natalie Portman was born in Jerusalem. She appeared in her first film when she was just 13. She has since starred in many famous films, including *Star Wars: Attack of the Clones* and *The Other Boleyn Girl*. On stage, she has played the title role in *The Diary of Anne Frank*.

Language

Israel has two official languages. One is Hebrew, an ancient language spoken by most of the Jewish population. The other is Arabic, which is spoken by Israeli Arabs. Many people also speak English, which is the most common foreign language taught in schools. Other languages are also spoken in Israel – for example, many immigrant Israelis still use the language of the land where they were born, such as Russian, Polish or Amharic (Ethiopian).

Sport

Football and basketball are the most popular sports in Israel. The national team has qualified for the football World Cup only once, in 1970. Club side Maccabi Tel Aviv have been European basketball champions five times. But other sports have brought even more success. Israeli athletes have won seven Olympic medals, including a bronze in the 2008 Beijing Games. In 2009, the national tennis team reached the semi-finals of the Davis Cup after a shock defeat of Russia.

IT'S A FACT!

Most Jews only eat food that is kosher (Hebrew for 'proper' or 'fit'). Kosher food conforms to Jewish religious rules. Meat animals must be killed in a special way and drained of all blood. Pork and shellfish are forbidden, because they are believed to be unclean. Dairy products such as milk must not be eaten with meat. Bread must not be baked on the Sabbath (the day for rest and worship).

◀ *Tel Aviv's basketball team, the Maccabi (in yellow), have topped the European basketball league on five occasions.*

Economy and trade

In 1948, Israel was a poor country with little industry and not much land that could be used for farming. Since then, it has grown into one of the most advanced and successful economies in the region. Most Israelis have a high standard of living.

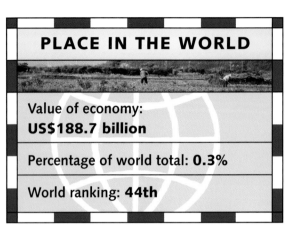

PLACE IN THE WORLD

Value of economy: **US$188.7 billion**

Percentage of world total: **0.3%**

World ranking: **44th**

Industry

Israeli factories make many valuable goods, from paper and plastics to computer software and pharmaceuticals. However, the country has few natural resources, and many raw materials such as oil have to be imported from other countries. The most important part of Israel's economy is the service industry, which produces services rather than goods. These include government services (such as education and housing), transport and tourism.

▼ *This man is working at a pharmaceutical factory in Jerusalem. Goods such as medicines are made in Israel and exported to other countries.*

▼ *Farming is bringing more money into the economy, as new irrigation techniques allow more land to be cultivated.*

IT STARTED HERE

Pill camera

The M2A capsule was invented and developed in Israel in 2001. It looks just like an ordinary pill, but contains a tiny camera. When a patient swallows the capsule, the camera takes colour images from inside the body. These pictures help doctors to spot early signs of cancer and other diseases.

Farming

One of the main aims of Israel's founders was to grow enough food to feed the population. Since 1948, the amount of land used for farming has tripled. New irrigation systems bringing water to the crops, and modern machinery and fertilizers, have allowed Israelis to produce a lot more food. Their main agricultural products are citrus fruit, vegetables, beef and poultry. However, Israel still has to buy most of its grain from overseas.

Transport

Israel has a modern and efficient transport system. It has developed quickly to cope with the rapidly growing population and expanding industry. There are over 850 km (510 miles) of railway track, and 17,000 km (10,200 miles) of paved roads. Buses are a major form of transport, and Tel Aviv's bus station is the largest in the world. Israel has more than 50 airports, including two for international flights in Eilat and Tel Aviv.

▼ *Road and rail links are good across most of Israel, connecting the country's major towns and cities.*

▲ *Ilan Ramon was a fighter pilot who became the first Israeli astronaut.*

FAMOUS ISRAELI

Ilan Ramon
(1954–2003)

Ramon was a fighter pilot in the Israeli Air Force. In 1997, he was chosen to train as an astronaut in the USA. Ramon became the first Israeli in space when he took off as part of a Space Shuttle crew in 2003. Tragically, the Shuttle broke up as it headed back to Earth, and everyone inside was killed.

Trade with the world

Israel has few natural resources, so it has to earn money by selling its goods to other countries. This has been difficult because the neighbouring Arab states are mostly hostile to Israel because of its treatment of the Palestinians, and will not buy Israeli products. Israel's main trading partners are the USA, Belgium, Japan, the UK and Hong Kong. Most of the country's vital oil supply comes from Egypt and Mexico, and most coal comes from South Africa and Australia.

Support from the USA

Unlike many of its neighbours, Israel has a healthy economy, mainly thanks to the USA. Since the 1970s, the USA has lent Israel huge sums of money. Over half of Israel's national debt (the amount it owes to other countries) is owed to the US government. In 2007, the Americans gave Israel yet another loan, amounting to US$30 billion.

Government and politics

Israel is a democratic republic. It is governed by a parliament, called the Knesset, which is elected by the Israeli people. All citizens of 18 or over can vote in elections, which usually take place every four years.

Leaders and parliament

The 120 members of the Knesset pass laws and discuss the country's policies (aims and plans). They belong to several different political parties. The leader of the party with most members usually becomes the prime minister, or head of the government. The prime minister chooses a cabinet of members who take charge of the different government departments, such as education or foreign affairs. The Knesset also elects the president of Israel. The president is the country's head of state (like the British monarch), but has little real power.

▼ *The Israeli prime minister, Benjamin Netanyahu, votes in the 2009 general election.*

▲ *Female soldiers on the streets of Jerusalem. Both men and women do military service in Israel, although women serve less time.*

Keeping control

Israel is surrounded on three sides by hostile states that have invaded its territory several times. As a result, Israel has built up a strong military force, made up of the Israeli army, air force and navy. These forces have modern, high-tech equipment, some of which is made in the USA. Most Israelis have to serve in the armed forces at the age of 18. Men serve for three years, and women for 21 months.

Struggle to survive

Israel has had to fight hard to survive as a state. In 1967, Egypt, Syria and Jordan threatened to invade. The Israeli armed forces struck first, capturing four pieces of Arab territory (the West Bank, the Sinai Peninsula,

FAMOUS ISRAELI

Chaim Weizmann (1874–1952)

Weizmann was born in Russia, where he trained to be a chemist. He became one of the leaders of the Zionist movement (see page 14) in Europe. A peaceful and patient man, he helped to persuade Western leaders to establish a Jewish homeland. In 1948, Weizmann was chosen to be the first president of Israel.

the Golan Heights and the Gaza Strip). In 1973, Egyptian and Syrian forces entered Israel, but were beaten back. Since then, Israel has twice invaded parts of Lebanon, and bombed Iraq and Syria.

▲ *Huge concrete barriers have been built on Israel's borders with Arab states such as Egypt.*

Rockets and revenge

Israeli troops left Sinai in 1979, but they still control or occupy the other invaded areas. The Palestinians have launched terrorist campaigns to drive them out. In 1987, the First Intifada (uprising) saw violent attacks and suicide bombings in the Palestinian Territories. In the Second Intifada in 2000, rockets were fired from Gaza into Israel. In response, Israel began building concrete and metal barriers on their borders with Gaza and the West Bank to protect against attacks. In 2009, Israeli troops entered Gaza in order to stop the rockets.

GOING GLOBAL

Over 160 countries in the world have diplomatic relations with Israel. This means they discuss treaties and other matters, and have officials working in Israel. These countries include the USA, almost all of Europe, China, Egypt, India, Turkey and Australia. Over 30 countries do not have diplomatic relations with Israel. They include 20 Arab countries (such as Iran and Syria), as well as Libya, Bolivia, Pakistan, Malaysia and North Korea.

The peace process

Israel has had a long history of violence. Even so, there have been many attempts to make a peace deal between Israelis and Palestinians. In 1993, leaders of both sides signed an agreement allowing Palestinians to govern parts of the West Bank and Gaza. In 2007, the two sides began talks to work out a peace agreement. After the Israeli attack on Gaza in 2009, Israel and Palestine agreed to stop fighting, but peace is still a long way off.

▼ *Israeli soldiers confront peace activists in the West Bank. Despite efforts to resolve the issues in this region, the troubles continue.*

FAMOUS ISRAELI

Golda Meir (1898–1978)

Golda Meir was born in Russia. In 1921 she moved to live on a kibbutz in Palestine. When Israel was founded, she became a politician. She was first appointed foreign minister and then, in 1969, Israel's first woman prime minister. As leader, Meir encouraged large-scale immigration and the building of new homes. She resigned in 1974.

Israel faces a difficult future. The most important goal in the next 10 years must be to find a way of living peacefully with its Arab neighbours. Peace will help Israel to build up a stronger economy and a more stable society.

▲ *The West-Eastern Divan Orchestra was established to promote peace and understanding between Arabs and Israelis.*

A state for the Palestinians

The first step is to stop the long conflict between Israelis and Palestinians. Many people believe the best solution is to create a separate state for the Palestinians to live in and govern themselves. The state might be made up of Gaza and the West Bank.

GOING GLOBAL

The West-Eastern Divan Orchestra was founded in 1999 by Daniel Barenboim (see page 17) and others. Its aim was to help Arabs and Israelis work together and understand each other better. The orchestra's young players come from many parts of the Middle East, including Egypt, Syria, Iran and the Palestinian Territories as well as Israel. It has performed all over the world.

▲ *A bustling market in Jerusalem. Israel's population and economy are growing, and as trade grows, the nation may become wealthier.*

Before this can happen, though, Israel will have to remove its soldiers and settlers from the occupied territories, and both sides will have to stop their violence.

How will the economy grow?

Peace will certainly make Israel's economy much stronger. The government will be able to save a lot of money by reducing the size of its armed forces. At the same time, trade will grow with neighbouring Arab countries, and foreign companies will invest more money in Israel's industries.

Peace in the Middle East

There is an even bigger challenge – finding a lasting peace across the Middle East. Many Arab countries do not accept Israel's right to exist as an independent state. They believe that powerful countries like the USA are friends to Jews, but enemies of Muslims. However, in 2009 the newly elected president of the USA, Barack Obama, called for a new beginning in the USA's dealings with Islamic countries. Although it may take time, this could lead to a peace settlement between Arabs and Israelis.

Glossary

Arab someone who belongs to a race of people that originated in the Arabian Peninsula who are usually Muslims and speak Arabic.

Christians people who follow the religious teaching of Jesus Christ.

Druze a member of a religious sect that is mainly Muslim but which also shares some Christian beliefs.

economy the financial system of a country or region, including how much money is made from the production and sale of goods and services.

ethnic group a group of people who identify with each other and feel they share a history.

export to send or transport products or materials abroad for sale or trade.

Hebrew the language of the ancient Hebrews, a people who claimed to be descended from Abraham.

immigrant a person who has moved to another country to live.

irrigation supplying dry land with water by means of ditches and channels.

Islam the religious faith of Muslims, founded by the prophet Muhammad.

Judaism the religion of the Jewish people, founded by Abraham.

kibbutz a communal farm or settlement in Israel, where members share work and property.

kosher food that is prepared according to strict Jewish laws.

persecution harassing or ill-treating someone because of their views or beliefs.

pollution spoiling the environment with man-made waste.

population density the number of people living in a square kilometre or square mile of a country.

republic a system of government in which people elect officials to make decisions on their behalf.

scriptures sacred books or writings, particularly the Bible.

sect a group of people who have broken away from a religion or faith because they have different views.

terrorist someone who uses violence and terror to try to achieve their aims.

United Nation (UN) an organization of the world's countries formed in 1945 to promote peace throughout the world.

Zionism a movement that aims to establish a homeland for Jews.

Further information

Books

Crisis in the Middle East:
Israel and the Arab States 1945–2007
(Access to History)
by Michael Scott-Baumann
(Hodder, 2009)

Israel (Countries in the News)
by Michael Gallagher
(Franklin Watts, 2009)

Israel (Changing World)
by Susie Hodge
(Franklin Watts, 2008)

Israel – The Culture (Lands, Peoples, & Cultures)
by Debbie Smith
(Crabtree Books, 2008)

Websites

www.cyberschoolbus.un.org
United Nations information site on countries of
the world.

www.factsofisrael.com
Basic facts, figures, history and lots of other
information about Israel.

www.jewishvirtuallibrary.org/jsource/israel
An encyclopedia of Jewish culture and history.

www.israelemb.org/kids
A site specially for children run by the Israeli Embassy
in the USA.

www.israelvisit.co.il
Take a virtual visit to the country.

www.mfa.gov.il/MFA/Facts
Israeli government site with loads of information.

Every effort has been made by the publisher to ensure
that these websites contain no inappropriate or offensive
material. However, because of the nature of the Internet,
it is impossible to guarantee that the content of these sites
will not be altered. We strongly advise that Internet access
is supervised by a responsible adult.

Index

Numbers in **bold** indicate pictures

A
Arabs 4, 5, 6, 12, **12**, 13, 15, 16, 17, 18, 23, 26, 28, 29
armed forces **6**, 12, **12**, 25, **25**, **27**, 29
B
Barenboim, Daniel 17, **17**, 28
C
Christians 16, **16**
climate 9
Coastal Plain 8, 12
crops 10, 11, 21, **21**
D
Dead Sea **5**, 9, 10, 11
deserts 4, **5**, 8, 9, **9**, 12
Dome of the Rock **14**
Druze 16
E
economy 20, 23, 28, 29
education 17, **18**, 20, 24
Egypt 4, 23, 25, 26, 28
Eilat 22
environmental issues 11
Europe 7, 14, 15, 17, 25, 26
F
factories 11, **11**, 20
farming 8, 10, 11, 16, 20, 21, **21**
food 15, 16, 19, 21
G
Gaza Strip 4, 12, 17, 25, 26, 27, 28
Germany 14, 15
Golan Heights 25
government 20, 24, 29
H
Haifa 8, **8**, 13
healthcare 15, 16

highlands 8, 9
housing 15, 16, 20
I
immigrants 7, **7**, 12, 14, 15, 16, 18, 27
industry 8, 11, **11**, 13, 20, 22, 29
Iran 26, 28
irrigation 11, 21
J
Jerusalem 6, 13, **14**, **16**, 18, **25**, **29**
Jews 5, 7, 12, 13, 14, 15, **15**, 16, 17, 18, **18**, 19, 29
jobs 15, 16
Jordan 4, 25
Jordan River 10, **10**
K
khamsin 9
kibbutz 16, 27
L
languages 7, 16, 17, 18
Lebanon 4, 25
M
Masada **5**
Meir, Golda 27
mountains 4, 8, 9
Muslims 4, 16, 29
N
natural resources 20, 23
Negev Desert 8, 9, **9**, 12
O
Obama, Barack 29
oil 20, 23
P
Palestine 5, 6, 7, 14, 16, 27
Palestinian Territories 4, 12, 28, 29
Palestinians 6, 12, 17, 23, 26, 27, 28

peace process 27, 28, 29
population 12, 13, 15, 16, 21, 22
Portman, Natalie 18
president 24, 25
prime minister 24, **24**, 27
R
Ramon, Ilan 23, 23
Russia 14, 15, 19, 27
S
Sderot **6**
Sea of Galilee 10, **10**
Sinai Peninsula 25, 26
Soviet Union 14, 15
sport 19, **19**
Syria 4, 25, 26, 28
T
Tel Aviv 13, **13**, 19, 22
tourism 20
trade 8, 23
transport 20, 22, **22**
U
UK 15, 23
United Nations (UN) 13
USA 6, 14, 15, **15**, 17, 23, 25, 26, 29
W
water 10, 11
Weizmann, Chaim 25
West Bank 4, 12, 17, 25, 26, 27, **27**, 28
West-Eastern Divan Orchestra 17, 28, **28**
Western Wall **14**
Z
Zionist movement 14, 25